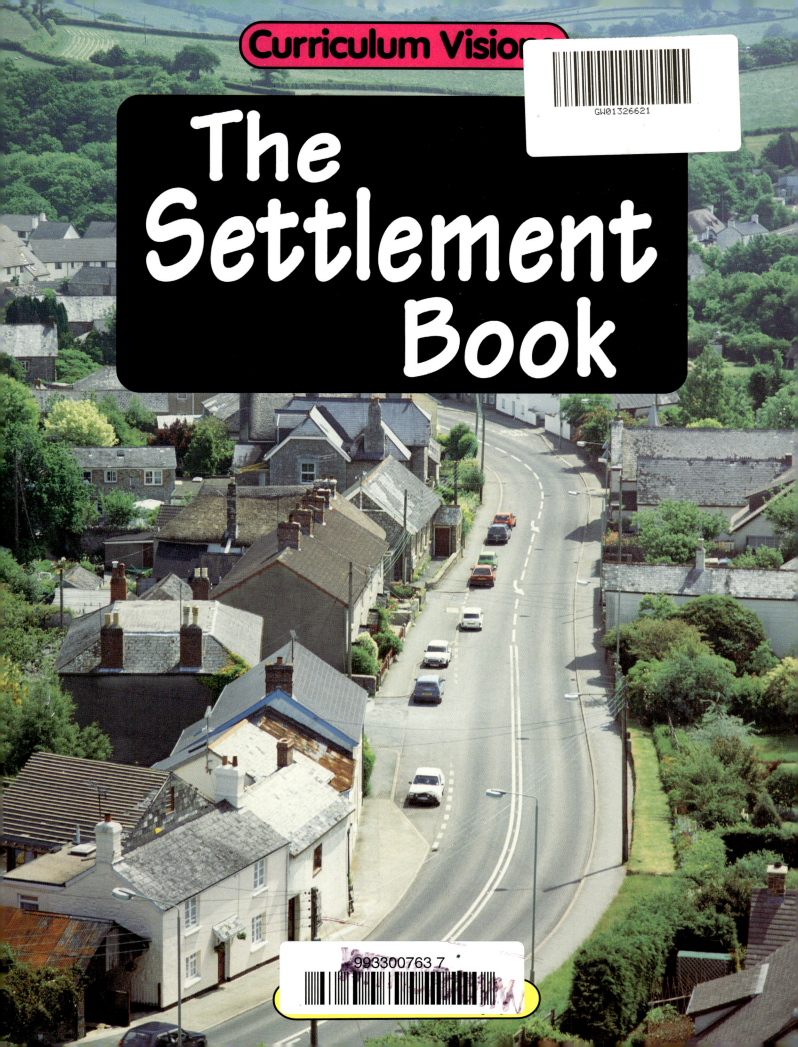

Curriculum Visions

The Settlement Book

A CVP Book
Copyright © 1999–2007 Earthscape

First reprint 2003. Second reprint 2005. Third reprint 2007.

The right of Brian Knapp to be identified as the author of this work has been asserted by him in accordance with the Copyright, Designs and Patents Act 1988.

All rights reserved. No part of this publication may be reproduced, stored in a retrieval system, or transmitted in any form or by any means, electronic, mechanical, photocopying, recording or otherwise, without prior permission of the copyright holder.

Author
Brian Knapp, BSc, PhD
Art Director
Duncan McCrae, BSc
Editors
Elizabeth Walker, BA and Mary Sanders, BSc
Page layout
Duncan McCrae and Mark Palmer
Designed and produced by
EARTHSCAPE
Reproduced in Malaysia by
Global Colour
Printed and bound in Hong Kong by
WKT Company Ltd
**The Settlement (Places) Book
– Curriculum Visions
A CIP record for this book is available from the British Library**
ISBN 978 1 86214 007 3 Hardback
ISBN 978 1 86214 012 7 Paperback

Illustrations
All illustrations by *David Woodroffe* except the following:
Julian Baker; COVER, 25
Tom Patterson; 13 Old London Bridge

Picture credits
All photographs are from the Earthscape Picture Library except the following: (c=centre t=top b=bottom l=left r=right)
FEMA 20tl; *Leeds City Libraries* 42; *The Stock Market* 18; *University of Reading, Rural History Centre* 8, 43t.

This product is manufactured from sustainable managed forests. For every tree cut down at least one more is planted.

Skyscraper in New York

Curriculum Visions

There's much more on-line including videos

You will find multimedia resources covering the topic of settlement and many more geography, history, science, religion and spelling subjects in the Professional Zone at:

www.CurriculumVisions.com

Glossary
There is a glossary on page 46. Glossary terms are referred to in the text using CAPITALS.

Index
There is an index on page 48.

Teacher's Guide
There is a Teacher's Guide to accompany this book, available from the publisher.

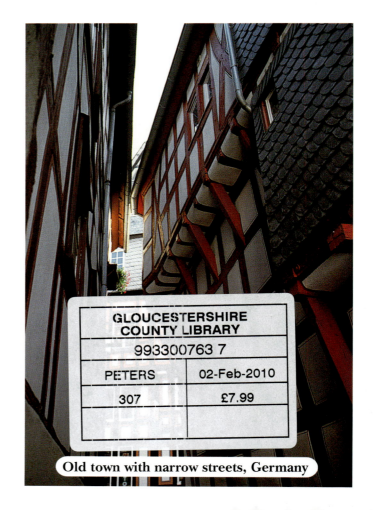

Old town with narrow streets, Germany

Contents

▼ GETTING YOUR BEARINGS
4   Where we live

▼ WHERE PLACES ARE FOUND
6   Where people settled
8   Where routes meet
10   Places in hill and valley
12   River crossings
14   Ports and harbours
16   Beside the seaside
18   Mines and power
20   Hazardous settings
22   Planned towns and cities

▼ FROM CITY CENTRE TO COUNTRYSIDE
24   What towns and cities are like
26   The centre
28   The suburbs
30   The outskirts
32   Country village
34   Roads

▼ CITY PROBLEMS
36   Growing into the countryside
38   Improving the city

▼ MY TOWN
40   Comparing places
42   Investigating the past
44   Where I live

▼ REFERENCE
46   Glossary
48   Index

Villages in France

GETTING YOUR BEARINGS

Where we live

Most people live together in villages, towns or cities. This is how we think about where we live and how we decide what name to give it.

We spend most of our lives in the area close to our homes. This might be a part of a city, a town or a village. Each of these places, no matter what its size, is called a **SETTLEMENT**, in other words, a place where people have settled.

If the settlement is large, we use our local part of it, our **NEIGHBOURHOOD**, for our day-to-day needs, and go farther away only when we want something special.

The way you view your surroundings will depend on whether you live in a village (picture ①), town or city (picture ②).

Wherever people live, they go about their day-to-day lives in much the same way. If you live in a big city, the streets around you and the local shops are really like a village.

▼ ① How you might view the nearby places you visit if you live in a village.

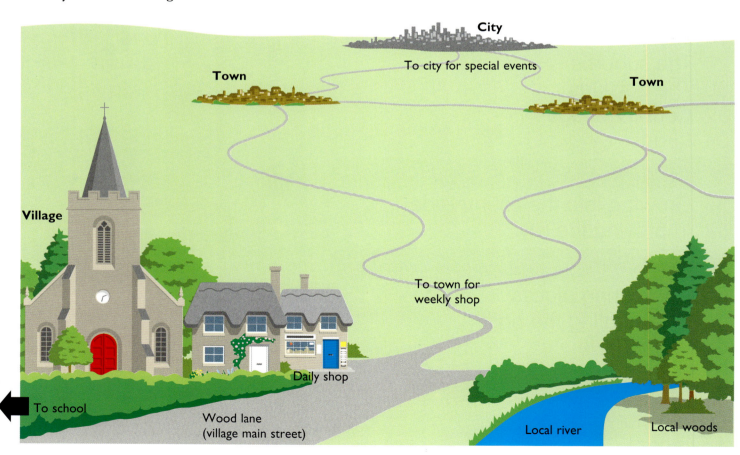

Weblink: www.CurriculumVisions.com

GETTING YOUR BEARINGS

Village, town or city?

How do we tell whether we live in a village, town or city? We may all have our own ideas, but geographers think about settlements in terms of what they offer in shopping and working, as well as by how many people live there.

A **VILLAGE** is a small settlement with only a few local shops and, perhaps, a doctor's surgery and a school. Most of the people who live in a village have to go to a town or city to work.

A **TOWN** is a middle-sized settlement. It has many more kinds of shops than a village. A town has a town hall and several schools, and may have a hospital. But, most important of all, it is a **PLACE** where you find many offices, workshops and factories. Most towns are also meeting points of main roads as well as being main stops on railways lines.

A **CITY** is the largest settlement. It is often made up of many **DISTRICTS**, each one the size of a town. A city may have a city hall and several big **SHOPPING AREAS**. There are large numbers of offices and factories, and, like a town, a city is also where many railway lines and roads meet.

▼ ② How you might view the nearby places you visit if you live in a city.

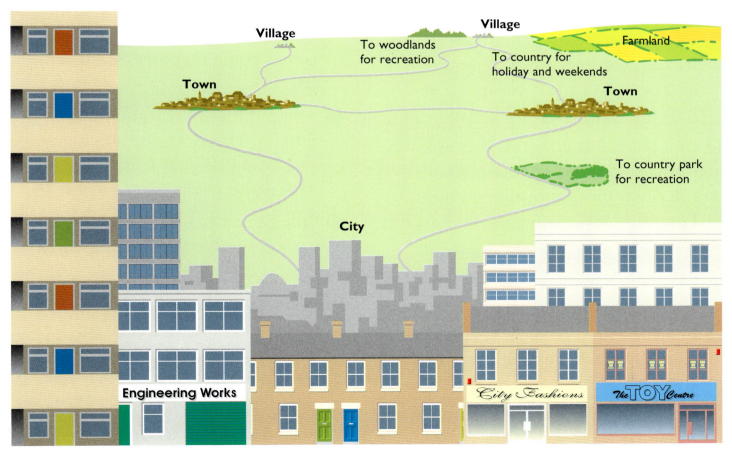

WHERE PLACES ARE FOUND

Where people settled

The place you live in today has probably existed for many generations. It may be big now, but it was small when it started. So, to see why it was founded, we often need to look at what people in the past might have found useful. Here are some of the most common places where people settled and why.

1. Along a **MAIN ROAD**. These were often stopping places for travellers in the days before motor cars. Find out more on page 8.

2. At a **CROSSROADS**. This is a natural trading place. This is shown on page 8.

3. Near **RAILWAY STATIONS**. Where goods are loaded and unloaded is a place for trade. See more about this on page 8.

4. Where rivers meet. Here, routes following valleys come together and provide a place for trade. See how this happens on page 10.

5. At a **BRIDGING POINT**. Rivers are difficult to cross. Different routes will often meet at bridging points. Find out more on pages 10 and 12.

6. Where an **ESTUARY** or wide river narrows. See these on pages 14 and 15.

7. In a river loop (**OXBOW**). The river could be used as a defence from attack. Find out more on page 10.

8. Among fields. Farmers needed to live close to their fields. This is shown on page 11.

9. On a **SPRING LINE**. This is where a spring produces clean water, perhaps near the foot of a slope. Some springs give warm water. These are called hot springs. This is shown on page 10.

10. At a **GAP** in hills. This is a good place for defence or for guarding a route, and is often a place where routes come together. See this on page 11.

11. Along the sides of a sheltered estuary. This is a good site for unloading cargoes from ships. This is shown on pages 14 and 15.

12. On the coast. A sandy beach gives a good site for a seaside **RESORT**. This is shown on page 16.

13. Where there is a **MINE** or a source of **POWER**. Mines need large numbers of workers. Find out more on pages 18 and 19.

14. Where planners have decided they need a modern **NEW TOWN**. More information is on pages 22 and 23.

Weblink: www.CurriculumVisions.com

WHERE PLACES ARE FOUND

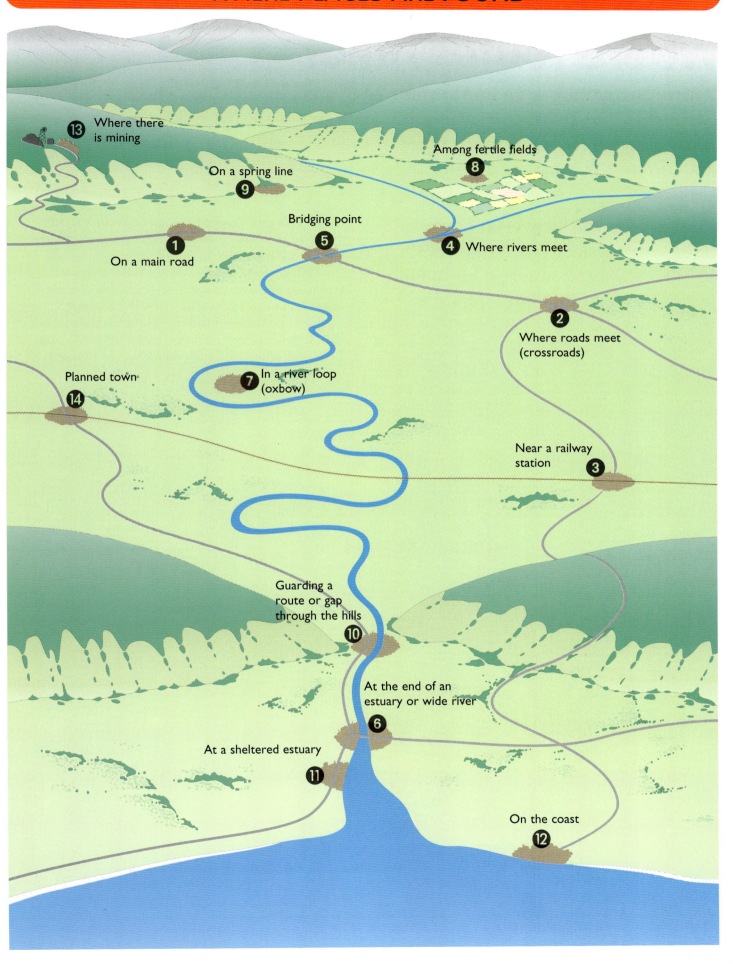

WHERE PLACES ARE FOUND

Where routes meet

Buying and selling is an important way of making a living. The best places for buying and selling are where it is easy to get to, for example, on main roads, and where main roads meet or cross. This is where many settlements grew up.

Markets were the **SHOPPING CENTRES** of the past (picture ①). They were the places where you could buy all of the goods you wanted in one place.

▼ ① This was a typical market place in a MARKET TOWN of the 19th century. Farmers brought their goods to sell directly to towns' people. Even by the 19th century, as you can see here, shops were replacing markets, and the original wide market street had been partly filled in with buildings.

The large building with the arches is the market hall. It gave shelter for some stalls, while the upper floor was often used for other kinds of business.

Weblink: www.CurriculumVisions.com

WHERE PLACES ARE FOUND

Crossroads markets

Railway stations and places where roads meet or cross rivers (see page 12) bring many people together, so they are also good places for markets to thrive (picture ②).

Many towns of this kind have a **MARKET PLACE**. This is a square or triangle of open ground where market stalls were set up in the past, and often still are today.

In the past, markets were not just for shoppers; business people also needed to trade goods, and crossroads were just as useful for this purpose (picture ③).

Some markets were set out along main roads. Sometimes, these are still called something like 'Market Street'. If the street is very wide, it may be called 'Broad Street' or something similar.

Shopping centres and malls

Open-air markets are a simple way of selling goods, but they are not protected from the weather. This is why shopping today is usually done in supermarkets or in covered shopping centres (picture ④). They still need to be where routes meet, which is why most places that were important in the past still thrive today.

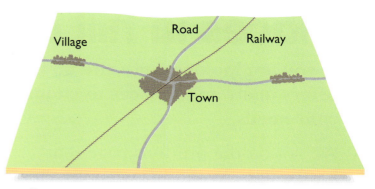

▲ ② A place where routes cross makes an ideal market centre.

▲ ③ Markets once existed for trade as well as for shopping. This old market was once used for trading cloth; today, it is a tourist attraction.

▲ ④ Many modern shopping malls are completely covered and have entertainments as well as shops and restaurants. This one has an ice rink in the middle!

Weblink: www.CurriculumVisions.com

WHERE PLACES ARE FOUND

Places in hill and valley

If you are looking for a site on which to build a settlement, the landscape offers many good places to choose from. Which you choose depends on your needs.

We saw on the previous page that settlements grow where people naturally come together, for example, to set up a market. Here are some of the advantages the landscape has to offer in helping people to choose where to come together (picture ①).

Riverside sites

A river crossing funnels people together and so is a good place for trade (see page 12).

Roads often follow valleys. The junction of valleys or rivers provides a natural meeting point (picture ②).

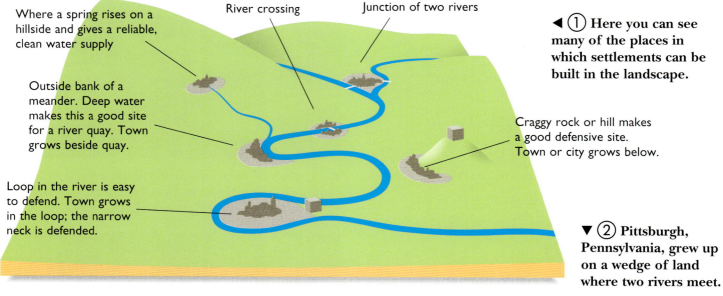

Where a spring rises on a hillside and gives a reliable, clean water supply

Outside bank of a meander. Deep water makes this a good site for a river quay. Town grows beside quay.

Loop in the river is easy to defend. Town grows in the loop; the narrow neck is defended.

River crossing

Junction of two rivers

Craggy rock or hill makes a good defensive site. Town or city grows below.

◄ ① Here you can see many of the places in which settlements can be built in the landscape.

▼ ② Pittsburgh, Pennsylvania, grew up on a wedge of land where two rivers meet.

Weblink: www.CurriculumVisions.com

WHERE PLACES ARE FOUND

The inside of a river loop (an oxbow) provides a natural place for defending your settlement.

Some settlements are built close to waterfalls and rapids for two reasons: the rapidly flowing water can be used for power, and the rapids or waterfall stop further navigation upstream.

Hill sites

Many villages can be found on hillsides where springs provide fresh water.

Hilltops and rocky crags are easy to defend (picture ③). Some spectacular cities have grown around such places, for example, Athens in Greece, Edinburgh in Scotland (picture ④) and Quebec in Canada.

Towns can also be built at gaps in hills to protect vital routes.

▲ ③ A village huddling for protection around the fortress, which was built on a knob of volcanic rock among fertile fields.

▼◄ ④ Edinburgh is founded from a castle that stands on a tall volcanic rock, making it very difficult to attack. It also presented difficulties in finding room to grow. This is why the old streets of the city have tall, closely packed buildings.

Weblink: www.CurriculumVisions.com

WHERE PLACES ARE FOUND

River crossings

One of the most common sites for a settlement is at a river crossing.

Wherever a river is crossed, people are brought together. Here, people can expect to get extra **TRADE** (picture ①).

A river may be easy to **FORD** or to cross by boat when the river is low or flowing slowly, but fording and ferrying are always slow, and impossible when the river is high.

Bridges are expensive to build, and they need to have good foundations and firm banks (picture ②). Without this, people look for somewhere else to cross, but where a bridge could be built, success often followed (pictures ③, ④ and ⑤).

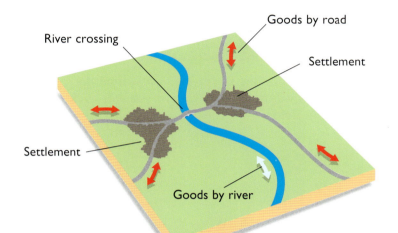

▲ ① This diagram shows how routes came together to make use of the bridge. Focusing traffic in this way gave extra trade to bridge-end towns. Often towns grew up in pairs – one at each end of the bridge.

▼ ② This picture shows how important river crossings have been in the past. This stately home (château) is built on the site of former castles that defended this bridge over the River Loire in France for centuries.

Weblink: www.CurriculumVisions.com

WHERE PLACES ARE FOUND

Rivers and trade

Boats were the main method of carrying goods in the past, and a riverside port was an important place of trade. The most favoured place for a port was as far inland as boats could reach. A bridge was normally put across the river at this point. Usually this was also the farthest place downriver that a bridge could be built. So here, traders going up and down the river came into contact with traders moving along the coast.

Some towns that were not at this favoured site, might build a bridge with many small arches to stop boats from going farther up river. In this way a town could make itself much more important.

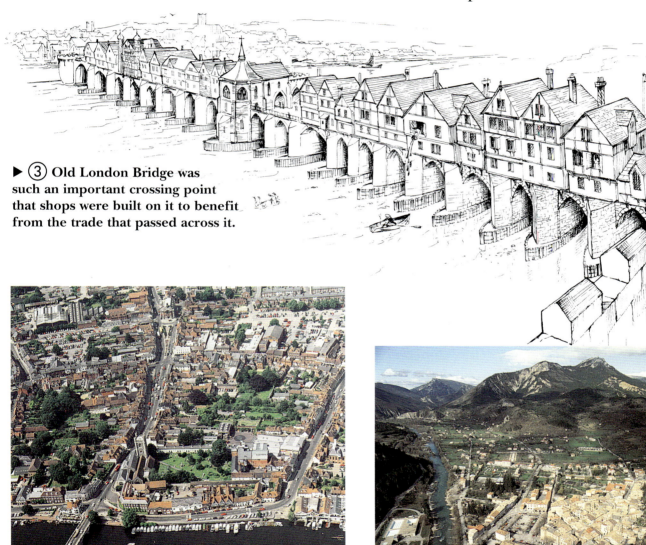

▶ ③ Old London Bridge was such an important crossing point that shops were built on it to benefit from the trade that passed across it.

▲ ④ Bridges can lead to trade. This bridge is exactly in line with the main street leading to the market street.

▲ ⑤ This bridge was built to cross a swift river where routes from several valleys meet. The town grew up beside it. On the right, you can see the remains of the town walls.

WHERE PLACES ARE FOUND

Ports and harbours

Some of the world's biggest settlements are ports. This is because ports bring in supplies that factories need. Ports and factories, therefore, often go together.

A **PORT** is a large sheltered place near the mouth of a river, or along the coast, designed to handle **CARGO** and people. It may have cranes, **DOCKS** and other means of making it easy for ships to load and unload quickly (picture ①).

Some **HARBOURS** provide natural shelter (pictures ②, ③ and ④). Elsewhere, artificial breakwaters – long walls curving out to sea – are built to make a harbour.

Many large ports are near the mouths of rivers, but inland cities sometimes have no alternative but to build a ship **CANAL** to get to the sea. This is why a ship canal was built to Manchester, England, and why the St Lawrence Seaway was built in North America.

▼ ① Some places provide superb natural harbours, as this view over San Francisco, California, shows. Notice the straight jetties (piers) for the larger boats and the curved breakwater designed as an artificial harbour (marina) for pleasure craft.

WHERE PLACES ARE FOUND

▲ ② Many small harbours take advantage of natural shelter where rivers enter the sea.

▼ ③ This diagram shows where ports are found. Notice that coasts with steep cliffs are avoided because there is little room to build factories or houses. See also the inland port connected to the river by a canal.

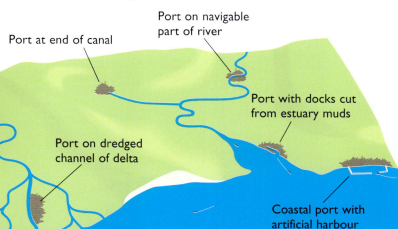

Factories line the docks

Many factories have been built in ports to use the supplies as they arrive from the ships. This avoids having to take large loads of raw material too far inland. Giant oil refineries, iron and steel works, and grain mills are just some of the many factories that use goods coming straight from the holds of ships.

The special shape of ports

A port needs a long stretch of deep water for loading and unloading. Berths for ships and boats may stretch long distances along a waterfront. For easy access to the goods they handle, factories and warehouses are built behind the berths. This is why ports tend to be long and thin in shape, rather than more circular, as often seen in inland settlements.

▼ ④ Liverpool docks developed in a river estuary to serve the transatlantic cotton trade. Over the centuries, the docks grew along the banks so that now they stretch for many miles.

Weblink: www.CurriculumVisions.com

WHERE PLACES ARE FOUND

Beside the seaside

Seaside resorts are very different from other towns because as much as possible of the town has to face the sea.

A place where people go to relax is called a **RESORT**. Before the idea of having a holiday by the sea became popular, hardly anyone could think of a reason to live next to a sandy beach. As a result, seaside resorts are often among the youngest of towns.

Seaside resorts

Resorts that have grown beside the seaside are very special. They need to be close to a sandy beach. As a result, seaside places spread as far as they can along the sea front (pictures ① and ②).

▲▼ ① and ② Seaside towns the world over have much in common. The top picture shows Blackpool, England; the one below is of Waikiki, Hawaii.

Weblink: www.CurriculumVisions.com

WHERE PLACES ARE FOUND

▼ ③ This diagram shows the places where resorts may grow and the kind of features to look out for.

Hotels, funfairs and other entertainments are found in the centre of most resorts (picture ③). This is also where you will find the holidaymakers and most of the restaurants.

People often retire to seaside resorts. They want to be close to the sea, but they are also looking for a peaceful time, and so are often happy to live away from a busy centre.

Fishing villages

Some seaside towns have grown up around places that were once used only by fishermen (picture ④). Usually, these are very different from resorts.

The fishermen needed a harbour, so they chose sheltered sites, for example, where a river flows into the sea, so fishing villages were often made of huddles of small homes in narrow lanes with no spare space to grow bigger.

Because the old centre cannot grow, and because it is not easy for cars to reach it, most of the new houses and hotels have been built on nearby cliff tops.

▲ ④ This small fishing village still has a few fishermen making a living, but most of the boats in the harbour are pleasure craft, and most of the houses are used by holidaymakers.

Weblink: www.CurriculumVisions.com

WHERE PLACES ARE FOUND

Mines and power

When people mine for materials, or use water power directly to power machines, they have no choice of where to build their towns. They simply have to make the best of the landscape. Sometimes this causes towns to be sited in difficult places.

You might think that few people would want to build in a valley with steep sides, where there is little space for building. But, there are two important reasons why so many towns are found in just such unpromising places (picture ①).

▼ ① People who mine know that they have to go to where the rocks and minerals are, even if it means building a settlement from nothing, out in the middle of a desert. This is what they had to do for this copper mine at Mt Isa, Australia. This picture, taken from the air, shows the mine. You can see the edge of the town at the bottom of the picture.

WHERE PLACES ARE FOUND

Mines and quarries

Some of the most important things that people need come from the ground. These are called **RESOURCES**. Coal and iron ore are the most common resources that are mined, but stone (picture ②) and precious metals such as lead, copper, diamonds and gold have also caused the growth of towns.

Mining towns have to be built close to the mines.

It so happens that many of the rich veins of metals and coal are found in mountainous areas, which is why mining settlements have to grow among steep hillsides (pictures ③ and ④).

Water power

Water is an important source of **POWER**. In the past, many industries were founded beside a waterfall or a fast-flowing river, which could be used as a source of water power for turning wheels and for driving machines. Many textile mills, and even metal-working factories, grew up in just such places.

▲ ② The people who work in this quarry live mainly in the village which can be seen on the quarry rim.

▼ ③ When mines and factories have to be built in steep-sided valleys, they often use up all the flat land at the bottom of the valley, and houses have to be built on the steep hillsides.

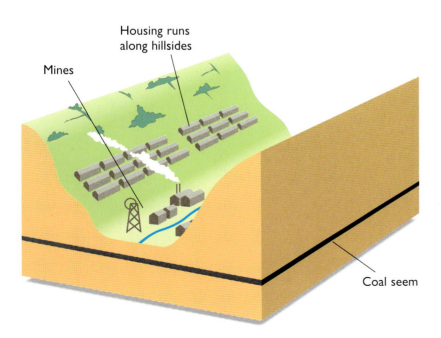

▲ ④ The Rhondda Valley in South Wales is typical of the deep valleys in which coal mines sometimes had to be built. The shape of the valley has clearly shaped the town. This historic picture shows the valley when the mines were still open.

Weblink: www.CurriculumVisions.com

WHERE PLACES ARE FOUND

Hazardous settings

Sometimes people live in places that put them at risk. Here you can see some of the hazards that these people have to face.

People often put up with **NATURAL HAZARDS** because, on balance, the good features of where they live are more important than the bad ones.

Coping with river hazards

All places next to rivers are at risk because, from time to time, rivers naturally spill over their banks and **FLOOD** the surrounding land (pictures ① and ②).

People wanting to live by a river (for example, to use it as a port) must look for areas of slightly higher ground. Most riverside towns and cities were founded on higher land. As they have grown, they have needed to protect themselves with embankments, called **DYKES** or **LEVEES**.

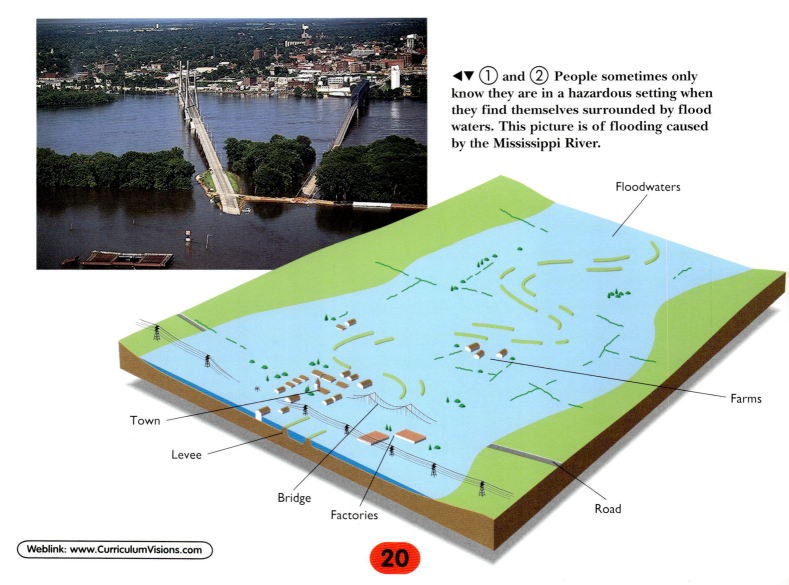

◀▼ ① and ② People sometimes only know they are in a hazardous setting when they find themselves surrounded by flood waters. This picture is of flooding caused by the Mississippi River.

Weblink: www.CurriculumVisions.com

20

WHERE PLACES ARE FOUND

▶▼ ③ and ④ Steep-sided valleys are liable to have landslides (soil), avalanches (snow), or rockfalls. The sun also rises late in hilly or mountainous areas, and so one side can be much colder than the other.

The land beside the upper part of a river is liable to flash flooding.

Land below cliffs and very steep slopes may be vulnerable to rockfalls and avalanches.

Land below steep slopes may be vulnerable to landslides or mudflows.

Coping with hillside hazards

Towns and villages built below steep mountain slopes can be at risk from **AVALANCHES**, **ROCKFALLS**, **MUDFLOWS** or **LANDSLIDES** (pictures ③ and ④). They protect themselves by growing forests or by building steel barriers on the slopes above.

Coping with coastal hazards

The sea is the most powerful natural force of **EROSION**. Many places built on soft rocks close to the sea have been washed away (picture ⑤). The only way to protect a coastal town is to use barriers of stones, called **SEA WALLS**, or long walls called **GROYNES**, that reach out into the sea and trap sand. These stop the storm waves from beating against the cliffs and washing them away.

▼ ⑤ Some coastal hazards

People who live in places built on soft rocks close to stormy shores may find themselves washed away.

People who live in places built close to where the sea and rivers deposit lots of material, can find themselves stranded from the sea as the coast grows.

WHERE PLACES ARE FOUND

Planned towns and cities

Some places have been laid out according to a plan. Every century has had its planned settlements.

The idea of planning what a town or city should look like is not new. The first city ever built, Ur in the Middle East, was planned and built five thousand years ago. The Greeks planned their cities, as did the Romans, the Aztecs and many other ancient peoples.

Most cities have some parts that have been planned. You can usually tell this by looking at the road pattern: areas that have the same pattern of roads were probably planned and built at the same time (picture ①).

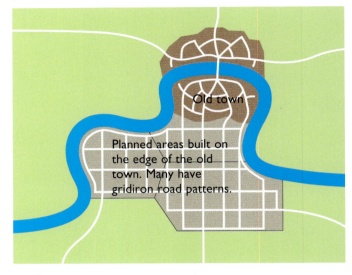

▲ ① The newer, planned part of a town or city can be seen through its regular street pattern.

▼ ② Washington, DC, the capital of the United States, was planned in the 18th century.

WHERE PLACES ARE FOUND

Planned cities

Some of the world's most famous cities were laid out in open countryside. The most famous planned city of this kind is Washington, DC, the capital of the United States (picture ②). Planning to use open countryside meant that it was possible to make the centre a place of grand **BOULEVARDS**, parks and public buildings.

Canberra, Australia, and Ottawa, Canada, are other famous examples of planned cities.

Planning to expand

Most **NEW TOWNS** and cities – even those built in the 20th century – have been smaller than the grand **CAPITAL CITIES**.

Through the ages, many landowners have laid out completely new towns on their land. They did so to make money, or to start factories and set up houses for their workers.

Some of the most famous planned towns are the 'cowboy' towns of the American 'wild west'. These were planned by railway companies to be next to railway lines.

Many of these towns have faded away and are now 'ghost' towns. Some of them survive as small places serving the surrounding area. A few have been more successful and have developed into big cities.

Modern New Towns and cities

New Towns and cities are still being planned. Many have been built in places where populations are growing quickly, such as in China (picture ③).

▼ ③ Some of the most recent planned cities are in Asia, especially in China. Here, they specialise in building towers that can house many hundreds of people. This is quite different to Britain, where New Towns mainly contain houses, not apartments.

FROM CITY CENTRE TO COUNTRYSIDE

What towns and cities are like

Most towns and cities are laid out in similar ways. Here are the parts of a city, what they are used for, and where they can be found.

Ⓐ City centre (downtown)

The smallest area of a city is the centre. The centre is described on pages 26 and 27.

① The centre of the town or city today is often the main shopping street. Find out more about the main shopping street on page 26.

② The town hall, city hall, civic offices, museum and library are shown on page 26.

③ Offices are concentrated close to the town or city centre, as you can see on page 26.

Ⓑ Suburbs

The largest area of a city – called the SUBURBS – is taken up by housing. See more about the pattern of housing in the suburbs on pages 28 and 29.

④ Older factories and warehouses are shown on page 28.

⑤ Older housing areas are shown on pages 28 and 38.

⑥ More modern housing can be seen on page 29.

Ⓒ Outskirts

This is a large area on the edge of a town or city. You can find out more about the outskirts on pages 30 and 31.

⑦ New housing areas. These are mainly on the edges of towns and cities. Find out more on page 30.

⑧ Factories that need large amounts of cheap space are described on page 30.

⑨ BYPASS, to keep congestion away from the town or city centre, is illustrated on page 31.

⑩ Out-of-town shopping centres need to be easy to get to, as you can see on page 30.

⑪ Reservoirs and water-treatment works.

Ⓓ Throughout the city

⑫ Main roads and railways. These are shown on pages 34 and 35.

⑬ Canals and rivers.

⑭ Parks, stadiums and open recreation spaces.

Weblink: www.CurriculumVisions.com

FROM CITY CENTRE TO COUNTRYSIDE

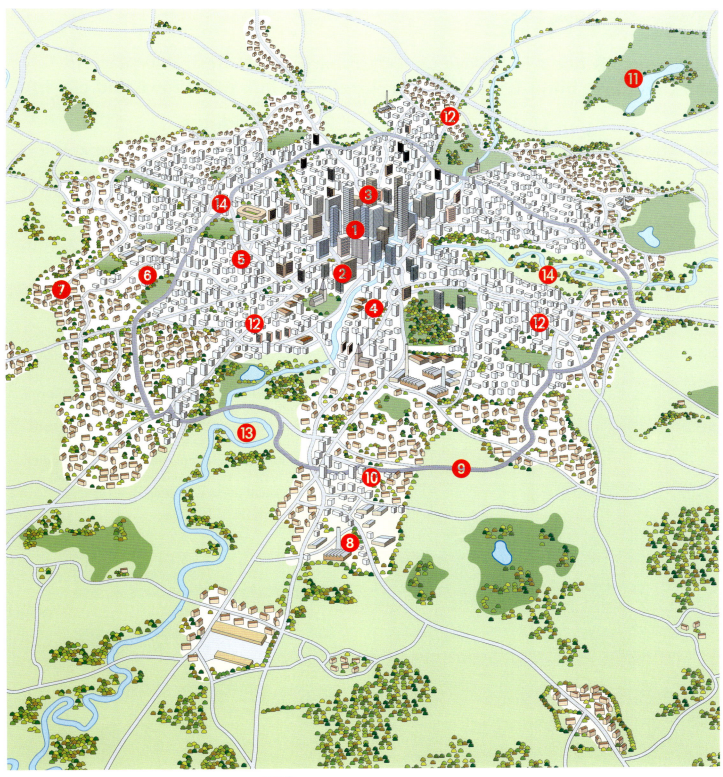

▲▶ These diagrams show the main part of a large town or city. You will find that the way the city is used forms rings, as shown here and on page 44.

Follow the changes in how land is used by looking at the side views, from centre to outskirts, shown on the next pages.

Weblink: www.CurriculumVisions.com

FROM CITY CENTRE TO COUNTRYSIDE

The centre

The centre is like a bull's-eye on a dartboard. It is a desirable place to work and live, but it is small. The centre is the hub of all town and city life.

Look around your town or city centre and you will find more variety than in any other area (pictures ① and ②). This is because you are where most of the main roads (and perhaps railways) meet. This makes it by far the easiest place for people to reach from all directions.

Public buildings

Think how useful it is to be at the centre of things. If you are in charge of the government with lots of workers, then a building in the centre is the easiest place for people to reach you, and from which to reach them.

◀▼▶ ① This side view of a town or city centre is the start of a journey through the city that you can follow all the way to page 32. In the centre you will find public buildings such as town halls and libraries; historic buildings, important religious buildings, department stores and other shops, offices, railway and bus stations, and usually small parks and other open spaces.

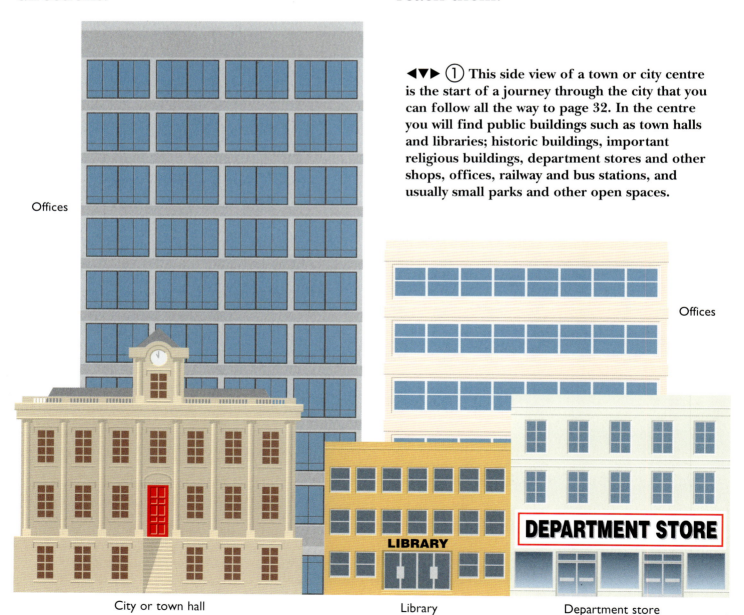

Offices

Offices

City or town hall

LIBRARY

DEPARTMENT STORE

Library

Department store

Weblink: www.CurriculumVisions.com

FROM CITY CENTRE TO COUNTRYSIDE

▶ ② This is an example of the great variety you will find in a city centre. Here, modern office blocks tower over historic buildings, while new forms of transport are used to carry people over the narrow, congested roads.

Shops

The centre is also where you will find the main **DEPARTMENT STORES** and many other shops. These shops offer a great variety of specialist goods from jewellery and clothes to sportswear and music. These items are not things we buy every day, and so these shops need to attract customers from all over the city. They do this by being in the easiest place to reach.

Offices

More people work in **OFFICES** than in any other kind of workplace. Offices can be many storeys high, so many people can work in a building that uses little ground space.

Having an office in the centre makes it easier for people to reach their workplace from all over the town or city.

To see what is in the suburbs, turn the page.

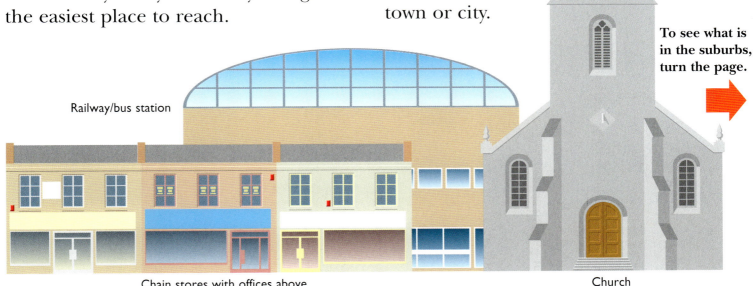

Railway/bus station

Chain stores with offices above

Church

Weblink: www.CurriculumVisions.com

FROM CITY CENTRE TO COUNTRYSIDE

The suburbs

As you move from the centre, land becomes more affordable and it is used mostly for housing.

Homes

Most of a town or city is taken up with homes. Places where there are mainly homes are called **SUBURBS** (picture ①). You will find older homes usually closer to the centre, and newer homes a little farther out.

In the past, people did not have cars or modern buses, and many had to walk to the shops or to work. As a result they wanted everything to be within easy reach. This is one reason why older homes were packed together in rows, or terraces.

The homes built farther from the centre were built in the motor age and so have parking spaces for cars. Most houses in this part of the town or city are separate family homes (picture ②).

Factories, workshops and warehouses

Although many people will work in the city centre offices, others will work in the factories, workshops, offices and warehouses that lie in the suburbs. Many of these workplaces are built together on **INDUSTRIAL ESTATES**.

Most industrial estates will be found along the main roads so that heavy lorries can move goods easily in and out of the estates, without having to use small side roads.

▼▶ ① This diagram shows the suburbs. On the left (nearest the city) are the factories and warehouses and the older suburbs and rows of houses. On the right are the newer suburbs, with more single-family houses and fewer factories.

To see what is in the centre, turn the page.

Weblink: www.CurriculumVisions.com

FROM CITY CENTRE TO COUNTRYSIDE

◀ ② This is a view over a modern suburb. Notice how the houses have been arranged in curved streets with many dead end streets. This reduces the amount of through traffic and makes for quieter and safer streets.

Shops

The shops in the suburbs cater mainly for everyday needs. Whilst you will find few supermarkets in the city centre, they are far more common in the suburbs, because people want to do much of their shopping locally.

In older areas, you may still find some shops built on the corners of streets. Most, however, are in shopping streets that are also on the main bus routes. Where there is space, shopping centres have also been built. Unlike high streets, where shoppers have to put up with the traffic, noise and pollution, shopping centres are protected from all but the most local traffic.

To see what is in the countryside, turn the page.

Blocks of apartments

Rows of houses

Single-family homes

Weblink: www.CurriculumVisions.com

FROM CITY CENTRE TO COUNTRYSIDE

The outskirts

The edge of a town or city may be a long way from the centre. This means that people may have to travel long distances to work.

The farther you go from the centre, the more space there is, and the more spread out buildings can be (picture ①). On the outskirts of a city there is room for **COUNTRY PARKS** and **LEISURE CENTRES**, for golf courses, out-of-town shopping centres, and for factories that use up large amounts of space.

Commuting

People who live on the outskirts of a town or city usually have the largest gardens, and often the largest houses. However, these people also have to travel longer distances to go to the shops or to work. People who travel long distances from home to work each day are called **COMMUTERS**.

Because travel involves longer distances, people who live on the outskirts of a town or city are more likely to have a car than those who live in the centre.

Out-of-town shopping

An increasing feature of the outskirts of a large town or city is the out-of-town shopping centre (picture ②). Because it takes more time and effort to get to this type of centre, and people have to make special journeys to reach them, so they expect more from the centres than from ordinary shops.

← To see what is in the suburbs, turn the page.

▼ ① This is the outskirts, which has houses, parks, and factories and shops that need large areas of land. Most of these places have to be reached by car.

To see what is in the countryside, turn to page 32. →

Country park

Out-of-town shopping centre

Weblink: www.CurriculumVisions.com

FROM CITY CENTRE TO COUNTRYSIDE

▲ ② This modern out-of-town shopping centre is designed to provide a pleasant place to spend a day, and not simply a place for quick shopping.

As a result, when out-of-town shopping centres are built, they will usually have department stores, speciality shops, restaurants, cinemas, funfairs, and open spaces where people can walk about in pleasant surroundings. All this, of course, takes up a very large amount of space, not just for the buildings, but also for the car parks that surround them (picture ③).

▶ ③ An out-of-town shopping centre with its huge car parks.

Weblink: www.CurriculumVisions.com

FROM CITY CENTRE TO COUNTRYSIDE

Country village

Villages are scattered throughout the countryside. Today, most village people work in towns and cities.

Villages are small places (picture ①). They have not developed into towns or cities, perhaps because they were not near enough to a meeting point of routes, or because they were simply out-competed by their neighbours.

Advantages of being small

Villages have less traffic and pollution than towns and cities. They have more space for larger gardens, and even paddocks for those who like to keep and ride horses (picture ②).

Problems of being small

Shops need customers in order to survive. A place that has few people will not have many shops.

The village store (picture ③) often has to be like a supermarket in miniature, offering all kinds of goods and **SERVICES**. But, village stores still cannot afford to carry the variety of goods that a big store can offer.

People who live in villages need cars because few bus routes go into the countryside. This can make life difficult for old people.

Commuters

Many people who live in a village have to travel a long way to work or school. Like people in the suburbs (see page 30), they are commuters. Commuters can help a village survive because, even though they live there, villages can be empty places if people are away all day. Now, with modern computer connections, it is possible for some businesses to be based in villages once more.

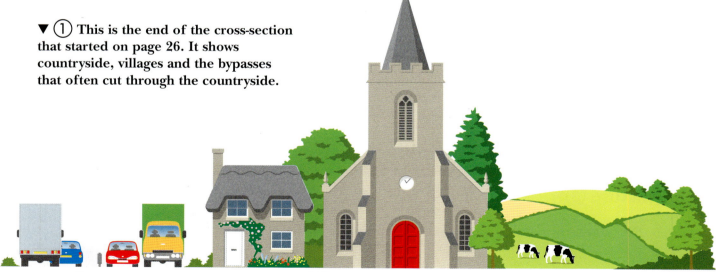

▼ ① This is the end of the cross-section that started on page 26. It shows countryside, villages and the bypasses that often cut through the countryside.

Bypass   Village   Farmland

Weblink: www.CurriculumVisions.com

FROM CITY CENTRE TO COUNTRYSIDE

Attractiveness

Because **RURAL AREAS** have not developed large numbers of modern houses, they may still have houses and other features that belong to centuries gone by. This might mean that the village is seen as 'attractive' and will attract tourists. Tourism can be good for villages because it brings extra trade and can help keep some of the services going.

▲ ② The historic beginnings of many villages survive. In this picture you can see how the village cottages were clustered around a stream. This was once a factory village, and the people who lived in the houses worked in a water-powered textile factory. Now, it is a tourist attraction.

▼ ③ A general store has to offer a wide range of goods if it is to survive.

Weblink: www.CurriculumVisions.com

FROM CITY CENTRE TO COUNTRYSIDE

Roads

We all need roads to get about in a city, but both narrow roads and wide roads can cause problems.

Both the oldest and newest parts of a city are its roads. The first buildings would have been laid out beside the first road; bypasses are often the newest roads.

Like spokes in a wheel

All places are connected by main roads (pictures ① and ②), each road going as directly as possible from one place to another. Each village, town or city therefore, has a pattern of main roads that tends to look like spokes in a wheel, with the town or city centre being the wheel hub (picture ③).

Roads that grew up naturally

Some of the oldest roads in a city grew up without any kind of plan. Many settlements first grew by simply adding buildings beside winding footpaths or lanes that followed the natural form of the landscape. These types of road have lots of winding turns.

Gridiron patterns

In most places, patterns of roads are now planned. One of the simplest ways to plan the road pattern is to build in squares, like a chessboard. This gives a grid of roads that cross at right angles (and so it is called a **GRIDIRON** pattern).

▲▶ ① and ② Roads are everywhere in this city. Notice that the biggest roads are those going in and out of a city like the spokes of a wheel and, those going around the city are like the hub of a wheel.

Weblink: www.CurriculumVisions.com

FROM CITY CENTRE TO COUNTRYSIDE

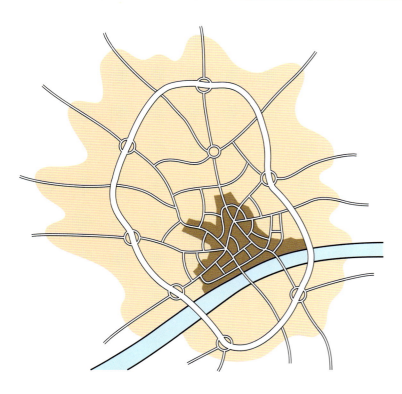

▲ ③ As towns and cities grow, so the number and size of roads increase. Here, you see the city as it was in the middle of the last century (coloured dark brown), and as it is today. Notice the inner ring road with its many roundabouts, and the extra roads that have been added. See also how much bigger the city is than it was a century and a half ago.

The exceptions to the gridiron pattern will be roads laid out for ceremonies. These big roads, often called boulevards, cut across all of the other roads in the city.

City motorways

Most towns and cities are congested with traffic. To try to separate out those who want to travel through the city from the people who want to get to the centre, many towns and cities have motorways. These have names such as 'ring road', 'inner distribution road', 'parkway' and 'beltway' (picture ④).

These huge roads can be useful but they can also cause harm to the city. Think of them as concrete rivers or railways. They are so difficult to cross that they carve up the city and make it difficult for people to get from one part of the city to another.

◄ ④ This is an aerial view of part of a TOWN CENTRE. Much of the housing has been built on a gridiron pattern.

Notice the ring road that now cuts through the housing, reducing the number of routes that people can take to get to the centre. In the past, there must have been dozens of connecting roads and paths. Now there are just two. Near the bottom right of the picture you can see that the ring road is actually wider than the river beside which the town developed!

Weblink: www.CurriculumVisions.com

CITY PROBLEMS

Growing into the countryside

Cities soon fill up. When people want new shops, homes or factories, they often look to the countryside nearby.

We need more and more space for the things that we do. For example, in the past, people were prepared to live in small cramped houses fronting narrow streets. Now we want to live in much bigger houses, visit large out-of-town shopping centres and have wide roads to get about. All this takes up space.

Of course, every time we want something bigger and better, we have to find the space for it. If there isn't space inside the city, then some of the surrounding countryside has to be used up (picture ①).

▼ ① **Here is a typical case of building into the countryside. To make way for this house, several trees have been felled.**

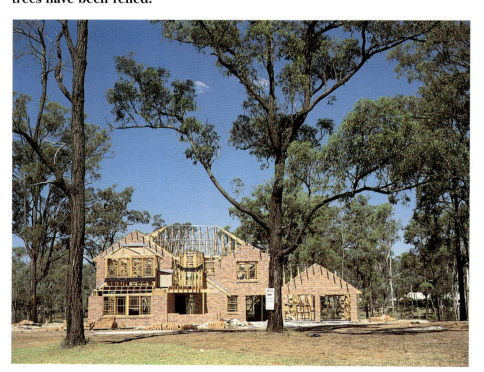

Sprawling out

The way towns and cities (**URBAN AREAS**) grow and grow is called **SPRAWL**. Sometimes nearby cities sprawl into each other, creating a super city or **CONURBATION**.

Sprawl often eats away at the countryside in a very haphazard way (picture ②).

Planners have been trying to stop sprawl and to encourage more use of city land. Sprawl not only uses up the countryside but it makes it harder and harder for city and town people to get to the countryside for recreation.

One way that governments do this is by creating a **GREEN BELT** around the city, town (picture ③), or even village.

You cannot build out into these protected areas of countryside without special permission. This makes people use the land inside towns and cities as efficiently as possible.

CITY PROBLEMS

▼ ② This picture shows a view looking towards a city from the outskirts. Look at how it is sprawling out towards you. The buildings are tightly packed together in the distance (near the centre of the city), but out here on the outskirts things are different, with large areas of unused land between developments of housing estates and an out-of-town shopping centre.

▼ ③ This diagram shows a green belt – a broad ring of land around the city. Very little building is allowed in the green belt.

Shopping centre

Housing estate

Weblink: www.CurriculumVisions.com

CITY PROBLEMS

Improving the city

How would you improve your part of the city? Here are some ideas of how to make city life better.

No city is perfect. Most have grown up bit by bit, with crowded roads and too little parking space, pollution, and areas that look run down. Even planned New Towns have their problems. In fact, it seems that a city can never be perfectly suited to everyone's needs. Furthermore, there simply isn't the money to put right everything that seems to have gone wrong.

If you had to choose what to put right, what would it be? Here are some suggestions for two kinds of improvement that people often want to see.

Traffic-free centres

Whether you live in a town or city, or are just a visitor, you are sure to notice traffic everywhere.

Many town and city centres have banned vehicles and have created **PEDESTRIAN ZONES**. Roads that were once main roads have been paved over, and trees have been planted to make city centre shopping a pleasure once more (picture ①).

▼ ① This was once a run-down chocolate factory in an equally run-down area of docks. The docks have been made into tourist wharves and the factory is now a shopping centre.

CITY PROBLEMS

How do people get to the centre if they can no longer use their cars? The old answer was to build multistorey car parks close to the centre. The new answer is to build car parks on the outskirts and provide bus or tram services to the centre – something called **PARK AND RIDE**.

Rebuilding old housing

Some older areas of towns and cities are run down and the people living in houses there cannot afford to repair them.

One answer was tried some years ago. Old houses were knocked down and tall blocks of apartments built in their places. Many of these **TOWER BLOCKS** were unfriendly places to live in and few people liked living there.

More recently, these blocks have been replaced with houses again, bringing neighbourliness back to these communities.

It is now generally agreed that older areas contain many fine buildings and that, with care, older areas can be made into very attractive places (pictures ② and ③).

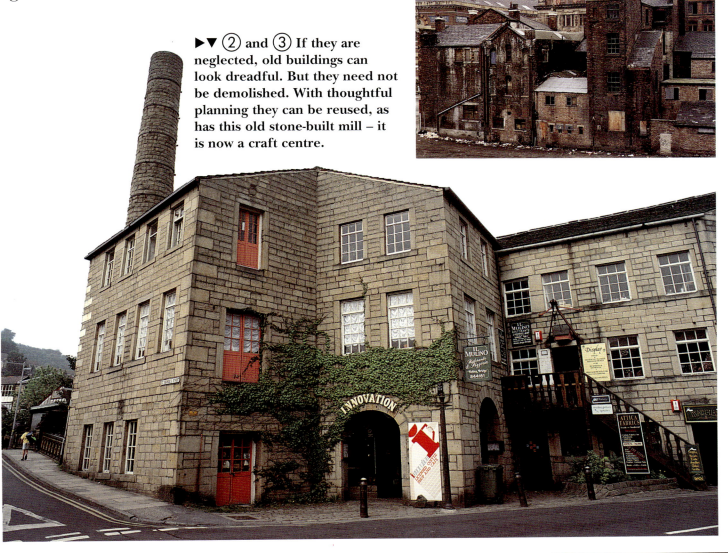

▶▼ ② and ③ If they are neglected, old buildings can look dreadful. But they need not be demolished. With thoughtful planning they can be reused, as has this old stone-built mill – it is now a craft centre.

MY TOWN

Comparing places

It can be very interesting to compare where you live with where other people live. Here are some hints on what to look for.

You know what it is like to live in the area where you have your home, but what would it be like to live somewhere else?

What is similar?

Many things that people do are very similar, as you will have seen earlier in this book. Every place has houses and shops. People go to markets, they go to school and work, and so on.

What is different?

What we tend to notice are differences rather than similarities.

Things look different because people have to make the best of the world around them. For example, if people live in a landscape with hills and narrow valleys, places might have a different shape from those where the land is flat (pictures ① and ②). Places built close to a large river might be a different shape to places built on a hill, and places built by the sea might be a different shape to those built by an estuary.

Places also look different because of their building materials. Houses built of creamy limestone will look very different from those made of dark grey slate. Houses made of brick look different from those made of wooden slats.

Places also look different if they are built for different climates. For example, a place built in warm, sunny Florida will look different from a place that has long, cold winters, like Canada.

▲▶ ① These are long 'street villages'. Nearly all the buildings lie along the sides of the single street. The houses all have long gardens: useful for growing vegetables in the days before supermarkets.

Weblink: www.CurriculumVisions.com

MY TOWN

Begin with a map

One way to compare the shape of places is to use a map. The map may also show more detailed differences, for example, a gridiron pattern of roads, or a winding pattern, or one that looks like the spokes of a wheel.

The setting is important

Most places have a long history. What you see around you is due to the work of many people in the past. To understand why they are the way they are today, you will need to know what is old and what is new. Then you will be able to understand better how the places have grown up.

▲▼ ② This is a compact village with a round shape. Notice how the houses are built close together and are separated only by narrow alleyways.

Weblink: www.CurriculumVisions.com

Investigating the past

Towns and cities had to start from small beginnings. Tracing back your town or city to its ancient past, using a map and information from your local museum, will give you many exciting clues to how it has grown.

Only a few towns and cities are new – most have long histories.

It may not be easy to spot the history of the place you live in unless it is a place where the past has been spectacularly preserved. In fact, many people think their town has no history. How wrong they usually are, as old photographs can show (pictures ① and ②).

There's much in the name

The names of places have survived down the ages.

Many town and city names hint at why or where they were founded. Bristol, for example, means 'the place by the bridge'; Leadville is a town founded to mine lead. Local museums, libraries and history societies often keep good information about local place names.

Roads survive

The first thing to be laid out in any settlement is its main roads

▼ ① Old photographs can give many clues to the way people lived in the past. Here is a street as it was meant to be used – in the age before cars!

MY TOWN

② Looking at old views of a town or city shows just how much it has changed. Look at how the factory chimneys and the factories dominated the town view a century ago. It is very different today.

(picture ③). The roads are, therefore, usually amongst the oldest features of a place.

The way to find the oldest roads is to look at the road names. Some street names that are usually old are: Main Street, High Street, Broad Street, Broadway, Market Place, Friar Street, West Gate, North Gate, South Gate, East Gate.

Roads that are named after distant places (e.g. Scotland Road, London Road) are also usually very old.

Churches

Some of the oldest buildings are churches. They were usually built early in the life of a settlement and so tell you where the settlement was founded.

Old maps

There are many old maps which show towns and cities as they were in the past, making it easy to compare them with a modern map and see how a place has grown.

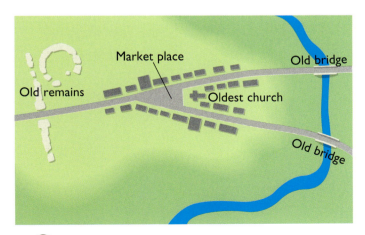

▲ ③ This diagram shows some of the things to look for in your town or city.

Weblink: www.CurriculumVisions.com

MY TOWN

Where I live

Towns and cities can look very complicated, so it helps to be able to compare them to a simple model, like the 'dartboard' model shown here.

How do you work out what is happening in the place where you live? One of the easiest ways is to make a simple model, which shows where things are commonly found. You can then use it, and the information on pages 24 to 33, to compare where you live with what generally happens.

Think of this model as a kind of dartboard (picture ①). The bull's-eye is the centre; it is small but easy to reach. Main roads and railways lead to the city centre.

As you go farther from the centre, the rings have a larger area, so more buildings (and people) can fit in. This is why the suburbs are by far the largest part of any town of city.

This pattern is exactly the same as that described on pages 24 to 33. Notice that the cross-section used on these pages has also been drawn across the top of the model.

It's only a model

Don't expect to find your local town or city looking *exactly* like this model. Most towns and cities have their own special shapes, but you can use the dartboard model to start you off on the trail of discovering what really happens where you live.

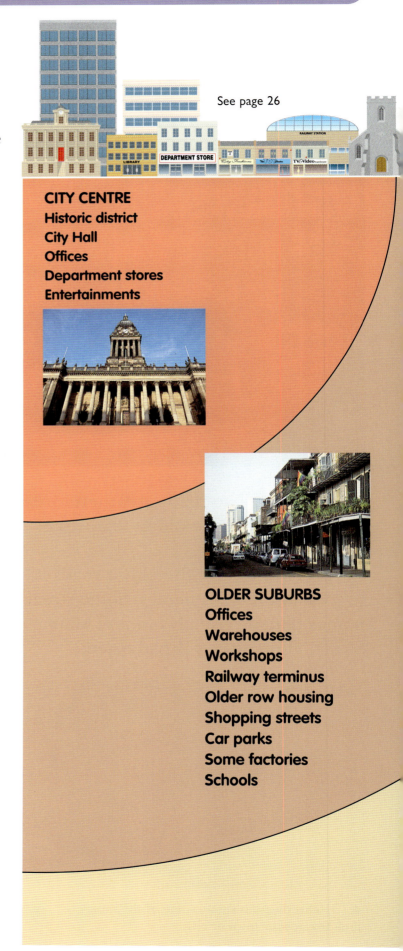

See page 26

CITY CENTRE
Historic district
City Hall
Offices
Department stores
Entertainments

OLDER SUBURBS
Offices
Warehouses
Workshops
Railway terminus
Older row housing
Shopping streets
Car parks
Some factories
Schools

Weblink: www.CurriculumVisions.com

MY TOWN

▼ ① This is part of a town or city model. It shows some of the things to look for in your town or city.

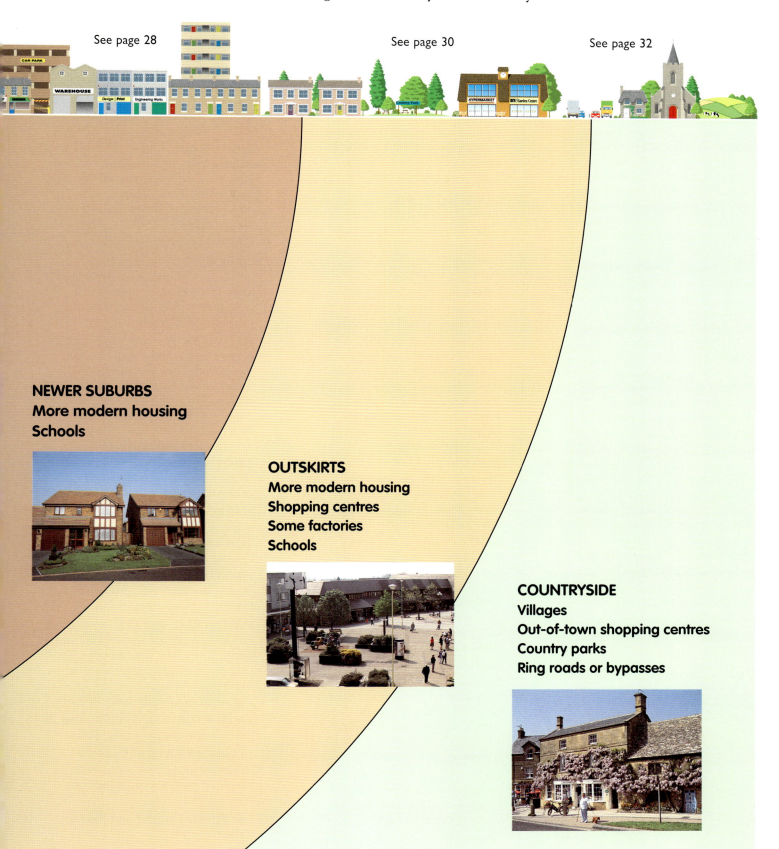

See page 28   See page 30   See page 32

NEWER SUBURBS
More modern housing
Schools

OUTSKIRTS
More modern housing
Shopping centres
Some factories
Schools

COUNTRYSIDE
Villages
Out-of-town shopping centres
Country parks
Ring roads or bypasses

Weblink: www.CurriculumVisions.com

Glossary

AVALANCHE A sudden downhill rush of snow.

BOULEVARD A long wide street or avenue.

BRIDGING POINT A place that has grown up where it is easy to build a bridge across a river.

People sometimes use two extra terms in connection with bridges: the highest point of navigation, which is the furthest that cargo boats can travel up a river; and the lowest bridging point, which is the closest to the sea that a bridge can be built (at least until recent times).

BYPASS A road designed to carry traffic around a town or city to ease congestion. A bypass can also be a ring road, encircling the city completely. Ring roads are used when the town or city is a natural focus for several routes. The world's biggest ring road is the M25 motorway around London, known as the outer orbital road.

CANAL An artificial navigable waterway. Rivers that have been widened, straightened and dredged are often said to be 'canalised'. Canals have the same purpose as rivers, to carry goods cheaply from one place to another. A port can develop on the banks of a canal as well as on the banks of a river.

CAPITAL CITY The city where the government of the country is found. It is not always the biggest city in the country.

CARGO Goods carried by any kind of transport.

CITY The largest size of settlement. A city has to be big enough to contain many separate districts. It is very difficult to be precise about what is a city. The term tends to be used differently by people in different countries. For example, a city in Britain is a place that has a cathedral, but this is an outdated and little used definition. A city in America is anywhere that has legally chosen to call itself a city. Geographers know cities as large places big enough to contain several divisions, such as boroughs or districts, each with its own government.

COMMUTER A person who travels a considerable distance to work each day. Most commuters live on the outskirts of a city or in surrounding towns and villages and work in the city centre. In the modern world it is very difficult not to be a commuter because shops, homes and workplaces are so far apart.

CONURBATION A very large city.

COUNTRY PARK A recreational area of land within, or close to, a large town or city. Sometimes a country park is created in a disused gravel workings, sometimes a former forest, or a former large garden.

CROSSROADS Where two or more roads meet and, therefore, where goods can be exchanged easily.

DEPARTMENT STORE A store that sells many different goods in one building. Most department stores are well known because of their size and the range of goods they carry. They are among the largest shopping buildings in a large town or city.

DISTRICT A part of a city that has its own shops and often its own local government. The word borough is often used as an alternative to district.

DOCK A part of a harbour separated by lock gates from tidal changes. Many big cities had, or have, docks. In some cases the city docks are too small for use by modern vessels and so the 'docklands' areas have been reused for housing and leisure.

DOWNTOWN A word for the town or city centre. The downtown area is often the same as the town centre or city centre, containing the main government buildings, the department stores, the tall office buildings, railway stations, and so on.

DYKE A long embankment designed to direct the flow of water. Other words for dyke include embankment and levee.

EROSION The loosening and removal of soil or rock by natural forces.

ESTUARY The mouth of a river valley. Estuaries do not contain deltas and so, with little dredging, can be used as harbours.

FLOOD The spilling of water over the banks of a river and on to the surrounding flood plain. It is unwise to build houses on flood plains unless protected by embankments.

FORD A place where the river is shallow and can be used for crossing. Most fords are only passable at low river levels. Fords were used in the days before engineers knew how to make bridges.

GAP A low area in a range of hills.

GREEN BELT A ring of land around a city that is reserved mainly as countryside. Green belts are designed to stop cities sprawling into the countryside.

GRIDIRON A city layout where the roads meet at right angles. Many towns and cities use a gridiron pattern because it is the simplest to design. There are some very famous cities where the centre is a gridiron. New York's Manhattan is probably the most famous of all.

GROYNE A wall placed in a river or in the sea. This protects the banks or coast.

HARBOUR Any place of shelter for ships. A harbour may be natural or artificial. A harbour may contain docks.

HISTORIC DISTRICT The oldest part of the city containing preserved buildings from past centuries.

INDUSTRIAL ESTATE A zone of a city restricted to factories and warehouses. You would expect to find most industrial estates close to main roads so that they can receive and send out goods easily by lorry.

LANDSLIDE A rapid movement of dry soil and rock down a hillside.

LEISURE CENTRE A place designed for people to exercise in and take part in mainly indoor recreation.

LEVEE An embankment beside a river.

MAIN ROAD A road designed to carry traffic through a city.

MARKET PLACE Part of the historic district in which open air markets were once held (and may still be held).

MARKET TOWN A town that has little industry and still acts mainly as a shopping centre.

MINE A place where minerals or fuels are extracted from deep underground.

MUDFLOW A rapid movement of wet soil.

NATURAL HAZARD A sudden and unpredictable natural event that could threaten lives or cause widespread damage to property.

NEIGHBOURHOOD A part of a town or city, smaller than a district or borough and more like a village in a town or city. A neighbourhood will have its own shops.

NEW TOWN A town built and planned as a unit.

OFFICE A place where people mainly work at desk jobs.

OXBOW A loop in a river.

PARK AND RIDE A system where cars are parked on the outskirts of a town or city and then the people take public transport to and from the centre.

PEDESTRIAN ZONE A zone from which all forms of motor transport are prohibited. Sometimes they are also called traffic-free-zones. In many cases, the banning of traffic has allowed a shopping area to be made more attractive, with trees planted, seats put out and some street traders allowed.

PLACE A general name for a settlement of any size. Geographers are often more precise and try to use the words town, city or village to give a better description of the size of a settlement.

PORT A place with a harbour where one of the main activities is the loading and unloading of ship and boat cargoes.

POWER A word for the rate at which we do work. Power is supplied by steam (through power stations), petrol (through cars) and so on.

RAILWAY STATION A place where goods can be loaded and unloaded and people can arrive and depart. The number of railway stations on a line is limited, so a station is an important item in the successful growth of a settlement.

RESORT A place built specifically to host holidaymakers.

RESOURCE Any kind of natural material that is needed by industry. Coal, oil and metal ores are all resources.

ROCKFALL A rapid movement of chunks of rock from a cliff.

RURAL AREA Another word for countryside.

SEA WALL A barrier designed to slow down the rate at which the sea erodes the coastline.

SERVICES A word for the jobs that people do when they help others for a living. Health and welfare and selling in shops are all services. More people work in services than in any other kind of job.

SETTLEMENT A place where people have settled down to live. Any kind of place where people live together. Cities, towns and villages are all settlements.

SHOPPING AREA A sector of a city where shopping is the main activity. Similar terms are shopping centre, out-of-town shopping centre, neighbourhood shopping centre and regional shopping centre. Each of these terms suggests a gathering of many shops. The other kind of shopping area is along a main road and would be a high street shopping area.

SHOPPING CENTRE A term often used for a part of the suburbs that contains shops surrounded by a large car park.

SPRAWL The outward spread of a city into the surrounding countryside. Sprawl is the kind of development that occurs without any planning, so that the land gets used up inefficiently. Planners are now trying to stop sprawl because it is spoiling the countryside unnecessarily.

SPRING LINE A part of the landscape where springs commonly flow from the ground and provide drinking water.

SUBURB A part of the outskirts of a city, made up mainly of housing. Geographers often find it useful to say what kind of suburb they are talking about. Then they use terms like poor suburbs and wealthy suburbs, older suburbs and newer suburbs, inner suburbs and outer suburbs. This is needed because the suburbs make up such a large part of the city, and housing areas vary quite widely.

TOWER BLOCK A word for high-rise apartment buildings, usually ten storeys or more. A tower block of offices would be called a skyscraper. Tower apartment blocks are much less fashionable than they were in the past, and many are being demolished.

TOWN A settlement smaller than a city and usually with a single central shopping area. Towns have centres of government and usually town halls. They might also have libraries and hospitals.

TOWN CENTRE The area of a town where the main shops, entertainments and government buildings are found. Also used when talking about a city centre.

TRADE The exchanging of goods.

URBAN AREA A part of the landscape where the ground is mainly occupied by buildings. Villages are still part of the rural area, because they do not use up much of the countryside. An urban area can only refer to a town or a city. Very large areas, where towns sprawl into one another, are called conurbations, meaning joined-up urban areas.

VILLAGE A small settlement. It has a few shops or other kind of services that are used communally. Thus, a public house on its own does not make a village. In general conversation, people use the word village much more loosely, meaning any small settlement that is not a town.

Index

apartments 23, 29, 39
avalanches 21, 46
Aztecs 22

Blackpool, a resort 16
boulevards 35, 46
bridging point 6, 46
Bristol, place name 42
bypass 24, 46

canals 14, 24, 46
Canberra, a planned city 23
capital city 23, 46
castle 11
chain stores 27
China 23
churches 43
city 4, **5**, 46
city centre 24, **26–27**, 44
city cross-section 24–33, 44–45
city hall 24, 26
city problems 36–39
civic offices 24
coal mining towns 19
commuters 30, 32, 46
comparing places 40–41
conurbation 36, 46
country parks 30, 46
country village 32–33
countryside **32**, 36, 45
crossroads 6, 9, 46

department stores 26, 27, 46
districts 5, 46
docks 14, 15, 46
downtown 24, 46

Edinburgh, a defensive site 11
erosion 21, 46
estuary 6, 46

factories 14, 15, 20, 24, 28, 30, 36, 43, 44, 45
farm 6, 20, 32
fishing villages 17
flood 20, 46
ford 12, 46

gap 6, 46
Greeks 22
green belt 36, 37, 46
gridiron pattern 34, 35, 41, 46

harbours 14, 17, 46
highest point of navigation 46
hill sites 10, 11
historic buildings 26, 27, 33

historic district 44, 46
history of settlements 42–43
homes and houses 24, 28, 29, 30, 36

industrial estates 28, 46
investigating the past 42

landslides 21, 46
leisure centres 30, 46
levees 20, 46
library 24
Liverpool docks 15
lowest bridging point 46

main road 6, 46
market place 8, 9, 47
market town 8, 47
mines and mining towns 6, 18–19, 47
motorways 35
Mt Isa, a mining town 18
mudflows 21, 47
museum 24

natural hazards 20–21, 47
neighbourhood 4, 47
new towns 6, 23, 47
new homes and suburbs 24, 28, 45

offices 24, 27, 47
Old London Bridge 13
old houses and streets 11, 22, 39, 41, 42, 43
old maps 43
older suburbs 44
Ottawa, a planned city 23
out-of-town shopping centres 24, 30, 31, 36, 37
outskirts 24, **30–31**, 45
oxbow 6, 11, 47

Park and Ride 39, 47
parks 24, 30
parkway 35
pedestrian zones 38, 47
Pittsburgh 10
place 5, 47
place names 42
places in hill and valley 10
planned cities and towns 22–23
ports 13, 14–15, 47
public buildings 26

Quebec, a defensive site 11

railway 6, 24
railway stations 6, 47
resorts 6, 16, 17, 47

resources 19, 47
Rhondda Valley 19
ring road 35
river crossings 12
river junctions 10
rivers 6, 7, 10, 11, 12–13, 19, 20, 21
road names 9, 43
roads 24, 34, 43
rockfalls 21, 47
Romans 22
rural areas 33, 47

San Francisco, a port city 14
sea walls 21, 47
seaside resorts 16
seaside settlements 14, 15, 16–17, 21
services 32, 47
settlement 4, 47
shopping areas 5, 47
shopping centres 8, 9, 24, 29, 47
shopping malls 9
shops 27, 28, 29, 32, 36
single-family homes 29
sites 6–23
sprawl 36, 47
spring line 47
spring line settlement 6, 10, 11
stadiums 24
suburbs 24, **28–29**, 44, 45, 47
supermarkets 29

tourism 33
tower blocks 23, 29, 39, 47
town 4, **5**, 47
town centre 35, 47
town hall 24, 26
trade 12, 47
transport 28

Ur 22
urban areas 36, 47

valley junctions 10
valley settlements 10, 19
village 4, **5**, 32, 47
village houses 32
village store 32

Waikiki, a resort city 16
warehouses 24, 28
Washington, DC, a planned city 22, 23
water power 11, 18, 19
where routes meet 8
workshops 5, 28, 44